In her beloved book *Feeding the Soul (Because It's My Business)*, Tabitha Brown helped us feel seen, loved and heard, sharing the knowledge she's gained from her own journey in life. Now, in this gorgeous keepsake companion journal, Tab invites you to think more deeply about your own path—and how to live in more love and happiness. Each creatively illustrated, uplifting page invites you to tell your story and explore your hopes and dreams, with thought-provoking writing prompts in Tabitha's encouraging voice and motivational and uplifting Tabisms to inspire you.

This soul-healing journal encourages you to take some time to reflect on your own sources of joy and hope, spirituality, self-image, and peace, and you'll return to this book when you want to appreciate what insights you've gained in your own journey—and just how far you've already come.

SEEN, LOVED & HEARD

ALSO BY TABITHA BROWN

Cooking from the Spirit

Feeding the Soul
(Because It's My Business)

A GUIDED JOURNAL

for feeding the Soul

Tabitha Brown

SEEN, LOVED & HEARD

WM

WILLIAM MORROW

An Imprint of HarperCollinsPublishers

This journal is dedicated to you.

I'm so proud of you for taking this journey.

I love you.

Contents

Introduction

Hello there! You alright? I'm so glad you picked up this journal, a companion to my first book, *Feeding the Soul (Because It's My Business)*. I know sometimes it's hard to fully process some of the things we read in the books we love, so I've created this journal to guide you in applying some of the lessons I've shared. In other words, I created everything in these pages with you in mind.

I spent plenty of time in *Feeding the Soul* sharing my own life and journey, but now I want to turn the tables a bit. I want to help you get back to you. Maybe you visit this journal every day, or maybe it's once a week. Maybe you only pick it up once a month. However you choose to use it, I encourage you to find your place or your season within this journal. Take your time with it. Find your page. See what page applies to you here and get to doing the work from there.

Nowadays, it's so easy to be distracted. Work, family, friends, social media, and the daily news can all be overwhelming if we let them. So what can we do to make sure we aren't falling apart? Well, honey, we can be intentional with checking in on ourselves. The one thing I know for sure is that if we check in on our hearts, minds, and souls regularly, we will develop a habit of doing so, and ultimately, we will get to a place where we are putting ourselves first. And you know Tab don't play about the importance of putting yourself first. You can't pour nothing out from an empty cup. Use this journal as a way to check in and fill yourself up when you need it.

Also, don't be afraid to walk away from a question or exercise and come back to it later. There is no right or wrong way to journal. It's not meant to be a chore. It is a gift that you give yourself in order to get to the best parts of you. As long as you do it, as long as you show up for yourself, you've done well.

Love you, Tab

1

That's Your Business

LOVE YOURSELF

LOVE YOURSELF

LOVE YOURSELF

LOVE YOURSELF

LOVE YOURSELF

LOVE YOURSELF

LOVE YOURSELF

LOVE YOURSELF

LOVE YOURSELF

LOVE YOURSELF

LOVE YOURSELF

LOVE YOURSELF

LOVE YOURSELF

LOVE YOURSELF

LOVE

LOVE YOURSELF

LOVE YOURSELF

LOVE YOURSELF

LOVE YOURSELF

LOVE YOURSELF

LOVE YOURSELF

Honey, I understand that for many of us, loving ourselves feels so hard and complicated. Mostly because loving ourselves might mean releasing people, places, and things we love so we can continue being who God has called us to be. But here's the thing: we have to love ourselves enough to let go of those things that aren't serving us well. Nina Simone said it best: When love is no longer being served, we've got to leave the table. Be willing to endure the temporary grief that comes with losing a friend, family member, job, or opportunity in order to get to the other side of the freedom.

Because freedom is the goal—you know that, right?

Free yourself from the mental heaviness that can come with having to second-guess yourself or doubt the intentions of people in your life. You have to choose you. You have to love yourself enough to say, "I deserve to be at peace. I deserve to be happy. I deserve joy, and I deserve to have that also within my circle of friends and family." And if you find that someone or something isn't giving you that peace, joy, and love you deserve, then you have to love yourself enough to let them go.

So let's check in with ourselves on this self-love thing. Figure out what it means. Decide what self-love and self-care look like for you and no one else. Because everyone is different. What floats your boat might not float mine, and that's okay. Let's dig a little deeper and find out the first time you learned your enough-ness. Or did you not learn that at all? That's okay. We are going to talk to our younger selves and help bring them right on along.

Spend some quality journaling time with these questions, exercises, and challenges. Follow up your reflections with prayer. And be clear: Consider that your prayer might not be for God to fix everything. Or for God to make things better (nothing wrong if it is, though). Just know that sometimes the answer to your prayer isn't either one of those things. Sometimes God might ask, "Why are you asking for Me to fix something that you know was not intended to be permanent? Why are you trying to make something be more than it is?"

And yes, I know that's uncomfortable. But honey, go 'head and work that out on these pages. You can be honest here, because that's your business.

Spend some time writing how the phrase on the opposite page makes you feel, including any challenges you have with it.

When you hear someone say
"love yourself,"
what emotions show up for you?

Take a pair of seconds to make a list of

ten things

you love about yourself. These can be physical things related to your appearance or body. They can also be related to your personality or the way you feel or think about things.

1. _____

2. _____

3. _____

4. _____

5. _____

6. _____

7. _____

8. _____

9. _____

10. _____

If you struggle with naming
ten things
you love about yourself,
write a little bit about why you think this is hard for you.

Now, for each characteristic on your list,
explain why you love that aspect of yourself.

_____

_____

_____

_____

_____

_____

_____

_____

love

Reflect on how those
parts of you
show up in your daily life.
Do the people around you see these authentic parts
of you or do you hold them back in some areas of your life?
How do those who love you respond to these parts
of yourself that you love?

Think Back
to Your
Childhood

When was the first time you loved yourself; that you felt like you mattered? I invite you to close your eyes right now and tap into the feelings of that memory. Now open your eyes and write about what you remember of that moment.

(If you can't recall a moment when you felt self-love as a child, that's okay. You can choose to write about another time or stage of life when you felt loved. Or you can use your imagination and write about an experience you could have today that would make you feel loved. If there were no obstacles, what would make you feel deeply loved today?)

In light of what you uncovered
about the first time you ever
felt loved,
write a letter to your younger self.

Instead of approaching her, him, or them
through the lens and from the perspective
of who you are today, try to speak to
who you were back then. Share words of
encouragement and love with
that version of yourself.

For many of us,
self-love
takes time.

We have to reprogram the stories
we've been told about ourselves and
the ones we've told to ourselves.

Over the next five days,
let's challenge ourselves to
change the narrative.
We are going to rewrite the script.

First, write three "stories" that play
in your head constantly that
you'd like to change. Example:
"I do not deserve good things."

1

_____

_____

2

_____

_____

3

_____

_____

For each of those three things,

I'd like for you to rewrite the script and turn it into something that better lines up with what it means to love yourself. Example: "I deserve the very best of everything."

1

2

3

For the next five days

Let's track how well you have replaced that old way
with the new way of speaking about yourself.

	I struggled	I improved	I nailed it
Day 1			
Day 2			
Day 3			
Day 4			
Day 5			

After Day 5, take some time to reflect on the following pages on how well you were able to shift into a new way of thinking and speaking. And honey, listen. It took years for those old stories to be cemented in your brain. It's probably going to take longer than five days for the new talk to take hold, and for us to truly believe what we've spoken. But that's alright, you hear? We all have to start somewhere. Now that we've begun the work of getting our minds together, and rewritten the stories we've been telling ourselves, let's think about how we might align our gifts, talents, and abilities with our dreams and purpose.

As I shared in *Feeding the Soul,* I've been performing since I was five years old. I always knew that I'd do something related to that, but it took some time for me to get to where I am now.

When you were a child,

what did you want to do when you grew up? What were some of the strong interests you had as a teenager? Does your current job/career reflect those early dreams? If it does, write out the story of how you were able to achieve that. If not, write about what has prevented you from pursuing those dreams.

_____

_____

_____

_____

_____

_____

_____

_____

_____

_____

_____

_____

UNPACK YOUR GIFTS

Everyone has gifts, talents, and abilities. Maybe yours are out there in the open where everyone can see or maybe you have hidden your gifts. Honey, go ahead and name those gifts God gave you. Can you sing? Well, put "singer" right on that big gift over there. Do you get joy from being a caregiver? Go on and write that in. There's something incredibly beautiful about seeing all the wonderful gifts you have.

Part of self-love is making sure we are taking
care of ourselves physically, mentally, and spiritually.
Honey, don't put your happiness in someone else's hands.

Self-care

means so many things to different people
nowadays, but let's get clear on what it means to you.
Imagine you are going on the most amazing date of your life.
Write out what would happen on this perfect date.
What are all the things this other person could do to make
you feel desired and loved?

Now, honey,

why would you leave something
so precious—*you*—in someone else's hands?!
What if you took yourself out on that most
amazing date? Rewrite your description of the
date so it is appropriate and doable for a
party of one. Add a little something extra
in there too, because that's your business.

_____

_____

_____

_____

_____

So what's the point, Tab?

Here's the point, my friend:

Give yourself the love you deserve.

And do it on a regular basis.

When we give ourselves the love we desire,

the love we deserve, only then do

we begin to draw the same to ourselves.

THE BIG LIST of SELF-CARE IDEAS

Let's make a list of all the ways you can implement
self-care. This way you always have something you can refer
back to when you "can't think of anything to do." And honey, make
sure you cover all the bases, including your mental health, your
emotional health, your physical health (yes, you're going to have
to get out there and move something), and your spiritual health.
Provide ten options for yourself so you can't use your budget or
time as an excuse. I've added a few to get you started.

Turn on your favorite song and dance
for 10 minutes straight. (Set a timer!)

Go ahead and have that hard conversation with someone.

Set aside 30 minutes to read a few pages from your favorite book.

1. _____

   _____

2. _____

   _____

3. _____

   _____

4. _____

   _____

5. _____

   _____

6. _____

_____

7. _____

_____

8. _____

_____

9. _____

_____

10. _____

_____

EVERYBODY
has a story to tell.
NO MATTER
where they're from,
what they've done—
GOOD OR BAD—
or what they do.

♥

Wait a minute! We are *not* done.
Now, you know Tab loves a challenge.
Can you

LOVE

on yourself for ten days straight?
I hope so. Because I'm inviting you to my

10-Day
SELF-CARE
Challenge.

For the next ten days, choose one thing
from your list to do for yourself
each day and record it here. If you want more
accountability, use #TabsSelfCareChallenge on
social media and post each day on your page.

Day 1

Day 2

Day 3

Day 4

Day 5

Day 6

Day 7

Day 8

Day 9

Day 10

At the end of the
10-day challenge,
reflect on how well you did.
Were you able to find some form of

each day?
How will you continue making self-care
a priority going forward?

_____

_____

_____

_____

_____

As you might have seen in the examples for the Big List of Self-Care Ideas, I made a point of including the act of having hard conversations. That is truly one of the hardest acts of self-love. But baby, it is so necessary if you want to be free. One of the biggest challenges we have with letting someone go is that we don't know what to say to that person or how to release them from our lives with love and grace. Let's work on that!

SAMPLE SCRIPTS FOR CHOOSING YOU AND LETTING SOMEONE GO

"I know that you love me and I love you, but I have loved myself long enough to know that your love is not serving me well. So I have to be okay with letting you go. I truly want you to go be great. We just can't be great in the same season anymore. This season has come to an end."

"I'm so grateful for the relationship we've had. We blessed each other in ways I know I'll never forget. But I also think we've both done all we can do to make this work. Sometimes it's important to realize when we've reached the end in a relationship and that's where we are today."

Your turn! Write your own script for how you might let go of a relationship that's no longer serving you.

_____

_____

_____

_____

_____

_____

_____

WHAT DO YOU VALUE?

Sometimes there's a direct connection between our ability to love ourselves and what we truly value in our hearts. In this image of the heart, write or draw at least four of your core values.

Examples: making money, having good relationships, being famous/successful, being physically healthy.

———•———

Now be honest with yourself, you hear? Because, honey, you are the only one reading this. Maybe it's true that you value external validation. You need to be liked in order to like yourself. That's a real value system that some people have. They need to be affirmed outside of themselves before they can feel worthy of love. But then what happens when you aren't liked or the applause has died down? Right. You will inevitably struggle to love yourself. So now that you've filled out your heart, reflect on your core values and ask yourself how they encourage/motivate/empower you to love yourself or not. What new values do you want to embed in your heart?

WHAT'S ON YOUR MIND?

JOY UNSPEAKABLE

JOY UNSPEAKABLE

JOY UNSPEAKABLE

JOY UNSPEAKABLE

JOY

JOY

JOY UNSPEAKABLE

JOY UNSPEAKABLE

JOY UNSPEAKABLE

2

Have the Most Amazing Day

♪♩ GOD's great JOY

JOY UNSPEAKABLE JOY

JOY UNSPEAKABLE JOY

JOY UNSPEAKABLE JOY

JOY UNSPEAKABLE

JOY UNSPEAKABLE

JOY

JOY

JOY UNSPEAKABLE

JOY UNSPEAKABLE

JOY UNSPEAKABLE

JOY UNSPEAKABLE

JOY UNSPEAKABLE JOY

JOY UNSPEAKABLE JOY

I know y'all hear Tab singing on these pages. Honey, listen. When I used to go to church with my grandmother, I loved watching everyone rocking and swaying in the pews or clapping their hands during all the hymns of praise.

"This joy I have! The world didn't give it, and the world can't take it away..."

Now ain't that the truth?! Joy is a choice. It's yours. No one can steal or take it away from you. So much of what I do to keep joy in my life is about focusing on it intentionally. Joy is my center! I'm intentional about keeping it there. See, I know what it feels like to *not* have joy. I have been to those dark places. I've experienced pain and heartache. And because of that, I made a promise to myself that whenever I feel myself slipping into anything other than joy, I will shift my attention and focus to the light. God gave me a second chance at life when he brought me out of my sickness, so how in the world can I not choose joy on a daily basis?

The truth is, I have bad days just like everyone else. There are certainly days when I'm sad or angry or upset. But part of the work is being intentional about joy despite what I might be feeling in any given moment. Sometimes, for me, it's just about looking around and finding something, *anything*, that brings me joy. And that's what I encourage you to do, too. No matter the circumstances we might find ourselves in, we all have a choice to focus on the good in our lives. To focus on the light.

Sure, I have bad days. I have tough seasons. But I'm alive to go through it! I'm alive to feel it. And so are you! There's something to be said about being grateful for even being able to feel sadness. You *get* to feel it, and that's a blessing all by itself. Because honey, we all know the alternative, right? We could just not be here anymore. But I am here. You are here. And for that, I am thankful.

Do you know how many people have called me fake because in their minds, there's no possible way somebody could be this happy all the time? That makes me so sad. I make a conscious choice to choose and spread joy–to make it contagious–because I truly believe we all deserve it. So my heart hurts when I realize how much pain some people must be in that they can't see my smile and laughter as something positive in this world. I want everybody to feel what I feel. I want you to feel what I feel. It is an unspeakable joy.

So let's figure out what joy looks like for you. And when you feel just a little bit of it, grab it! Smile and laugh and dance. I promise you, it changes the moment. It spreads like wildfire. Try smiling at someone at the store and watch what happens. Tell someone you are glad they are here and watch how their face just lights up. Even as you unpack what joy looks like for you on these pages, think about all the ways you can share that joy with the people around you.

What brings you joy?

I know that might feel like a simple question, but I want you to think hard about it. Be specific. Name at least five things that bring you joy and explain why.

1. _____

_____

2. _____

_____

3. _____

_____

4. _____

_____

5. _____

_____

Considering what you've just written, how might you expand your joy list? Sometimes we learn more about what brings us joy by trying new things, going on new adventures, or meeting new people. What are some things you'd like to try in the next few months?

New additions to my joy list:

Write out a plan for accomplishing at least one of these within the next ninety days.

_____

_____

_____

_____

_____

_____

_____

Now that you have a clear picture of what joy has looked like for you in the past, what it looks like right now, and what it will look like in the future, let's consider what has stopped you from experiencing joy. Take a brief moment and close your eyes. Allow images of your happiest times to unfold on the movie screen of your mind. What do you see? How does remembering that happiness make you feel? Very good. Now spend some time writing about what has prevented you from re-creating those moments in your life. What has stopped you from having more joy in your life?

joy

joy

TODAY IS ALL YOU
have for sure
anyway...
— and —
TODAY IS AS GOOD
A DAY AS ANY
to BEGIN taking
CARE of YOUR
BUSINESS.

Sometimes we have to truly see joy in order to understand what joy might look like in our own lives. With all the reflection you've done so far, it's time to create your own personal guide for reclaiming your joy. I'll show you mine just to give you an idea of what's possible:

Joy looks like . . .

Those *good* tears
Laughter
Sun kissing my face
Wind in my hair
Being able to move my body
Thinking about what God did for me

Your turn!

Joy looks like . . .

_____

_____

_____

_____

One of the things that sometimes makes it difficult to hold on to our joy is not paying close attention to our life. Are you reading the signs in your relationship, in your career path, or in your spiritual journey? Or are there areas of your life you know you are in denial about? Are there things you need to think about but are afraid to because of how painful it is? Baby, let's unpack all that right here. Name two situations, decisions, or relationships where you know you've been avoiding the signs. Then list what those signs are.

Situation, Decision, or Relationship

_____

Sign #1 _____

_____

Sign #2 _____

_____

Sign #3 _____

Situation, Decision, or Relationship

_____

Sign #1 _____

_____

Sign #2 _____

_____

Sign #3 _____

_____

Now reflect on your findings here.

Which situation, decision, or relationship has been showing you multiple signs? What does that group of signs tell you about your next move in that area? Why are you afraid of taking that first step?

HONEY, let it go

Take a pair of seconds and think about all the things you need to release in your life in order to feel free. (Yes, free! You do remember that freedom is the goal, right?) Does a person come to mind? A job? An opportunity that doesn't align well with your life? An attitude? What do you need to let go? Sometimes we can hold on so tight to something that's well past its season in our lives that we don't realize that everything we've ever longed for is on the other side of that surrender.

An open hand can receive; a closed one cannot.

let it go

Choose one or two things from your "let it go" list.
Write out a plan for how you might begin to let that thang go.
It doesn't have to be perfect. You don't have to be certain
you'll do it (yet). But sometimes you have to see a thing
in order to know that it is possible. That includes seeing
yourself letting something go, even before you actually do it.

dreams

Draw an image or sketch that represents any dream you
have. Maybe even turn these pages into a kind of "life vision
board" using cutouts from magazines and newspapers.
What do you long to do or be?
How do you hope to serve the world?
What is your ultimate purpose?
I'm not talking about your job, necessarily.
I'm talking about the dream you have deep down in
your heart that maybe you still believe is impossible.
The dream that seems like it's taking forever to come true.
When you finish drawing/sketching/collaging, spend some
time sitting with your images.

Pray about them.

Meditate on them.

Touch the image on the page.

See those images in your mind.
If you feel led to, write a little bit about how seeing
and sitting with these images makes you feel.

HOW MUCH IS IN MY CUP?

Sometimes we struggle to find joy because we have given too much of ourselves. There's not enough room for joy because we've poured out all our love and attention onto other people and kept nothing for ourselves.

Honey, some of us are plain empty!

As a visual exercise, mark just how much of your time, energy, and attention you give up on any given day. Get creative here! Maybe designate a color for each area of your life, like family, work, pursuit of dreams, and so on. This way, you can clearly see what you're pouring out and what's left in your "cup" for you. Reflect a bit here on what you learned from the previous exercise. How much is left in your cup? How does the knowledge of this make you feel?

ME | OTHERS

What are
three things
you can do this week or month
to ensure you aren't pouring everything out
and leaving nothing in your cup for yourself?

1. _____

_____

_____

2. _____

_____

_____

3. _____

_____

_____

WHAT'S ON YOUR MIND?

LOVE OTHERS

LOVE OTHERS

LOVE OTHERS

LOVE OTHERS

LOVE OTHERS

LOVE OTHERS

LOVE OTHERS

LOVE OTHERS

3

Don't You Dare Go Messing Up No One Else's

LOVE OTHERS

LOVE OTHERS

LOVE OTHERS

LOVE OTHERS
LOVE OTHERS
LOVE OTHERS
LOVE OTHERS
LOVE OTHERS
LOVE OTHERS
LOVE OTHERS
LOVE OTHERS
LOVE OTHERS
LOVE OTHERS
LOVE OTHERS
LOVE OTHERS
LOVE OTHERS
LOVE OTHERS
LOVE
LOVE OTHERS
LOVE OTHERS
LOVE OTHERS
LOVE OTHERS
LOVE OTHERS
LOVE OTHERS
LOVE OTHERS
LOVE OTHERS
LOVE OTHERS
LOVE OTHERS

All I've ever wanted to do is love on people. My mama used to say that I was like that even as a little girl. She was a social worker who loved people, and I know I got that from her. She told Chance when we first got together, "You got to be careful with her, honey. She bring people home. She like to take care of people." He laughed in disbelief, but guess what? He soon found out that she was right!

When I was little, there was a family who lived near Riverbend, our neighborhood in Stoneville, North Carolina. Behind the homes were these deep dark woods where this family lived. They were such sweet people. Never bothered anyone, and always kind when we saw them. They also didn't have any money, and I vividly remember that their doors never really quite closed. They had goats and animals coming in and out, and the children were often made fun of because their clothes and bodies were never clean. Their little girl was about two years younger than me, and she would come into the neighborhood to play sometimes. Even at that young age, I was observant. I noticed that she was always hungry. So what did Tab do? The same thing her mama would have done.

"Mama, we got to have our friend and her brothers over for dinner because they are hungry!"

"Mama, can she take a bath at our house? They don't have no water at theirs."

I'm sure there are those who would say that as a child, I shouldn't have been worried or concerned about such things. But sometimes God puts something inside of you that causes you to have great compassion for people. Even now, as an adult, that love and compassion comes naturally to me. When people hurt me, I can still love them–even if only from a distance. Loving them is a reflection of the grace and love I give myself. If I'm not willing to give of myself to others, then why am I here? As human beings, we are in community with each other. We didn't come to live in this world alone. We must be there for each other.

And loving on others just feels good. I feel so much joy when I'm able to love and give to others. When things are hard for me, I remember the power of giving and the many times I gave my last and it returned to me tenfold. My daddy always used to say, "Honey, if you give something to somebody, make sure that you don't need it in return. Make sure you can live without it." I don't want all the stuff that gets attached to giving when we get worried about "When are they going to pay me back?" I've already been paid back. The joy I get from giving is enough. I enjoy the feeling that comes with seeing somebody happy because you thought of them, because you made the effort to see them, because you heard them and you made it known that they were loved.

I'm a firm believer that God is love. And sometimes the only God a person may encounter in a day or moment is in the love I'm willing to give them. God lives and moves through all of us. Let's figure out how to intentionally show God's love to those around us.

Listen, honey,

there are seasons in some people's lives when they just
don't want to be bothered. Or they lack motivation to do
the things they want to do or live the way we want to live.
That's the hump they need to get over even before they
start loving on other people. I get it, so let's start there.
When I learned how to change the way I thought about
things when I lacked motivation to do something,
everything changed for me. I started to realize that it
was actually a privilege to be able to do anything that was
going to better myself, my family, or the world.

Make a list of things you struggle with doing for
yourself and then write a new script that acknowledges
your gratitude for even being able to do that thing.
I'll start . . .

The struggle	In gratitude
I really don't want to exercise.	I *get* to exercise. I have been blessed with the full use of my limbs, and I get to walk and dance and lift weights in order to be healthy.

Your turn!

The struggle	In gratitude
The struggle	In gratitude
The struggle	In gratitude
The struggle	In gratitude
The struggle	In gratitude

WHAT'S ON YOUR MIND?

LOVE

What does it mean to you to love other people?
Do you show your love in subtle ways or with more overt
actions? In what ways have you been able to show
your love to those around you?

_____

_____

_____

_____

_____

_____

_____

_____

We all have bad days.

No one should be judged by the worst thing they ever did. That said, part of loving on people is knowing how to apologize. How to make amends. Are there people in your life who need to hear your apology? Write their names here. Write what you might say to them once you build up the courage to have that conversation.

WHO CAN YOU

LOVE

ACTIVITY

Name five people

you can show love this week. Think about what
they need or how they might have been feeling
lately, and be very intentional about the specific
thing you will do or say that will let them
know you see and hear them.
P.S. Add your name to the list if you need to,
honey, because that's your business.

WHO?   HOW?

1.

2.

3.

4.

5.

Sometimes the hard part about loving on others, or even allowing ourselves to be loved, is that we have held on to too many secrets. Things that have happened to us, or things we've done that we are unable to let go of and that prevent us from living the life God would want us to live.
Write about one secret you are holding that seems to be getting in the way.

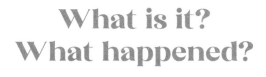

What is it?
What happened?

_____

_____

_____

_____

_____

_____

IS THERE
one
trustworthy
person

you can share your secret with in
order to lighten the weight?
If so, what would it take for you to
consider sharing your secret with
them? If not, what are some other
ways you might free yourself from the
heaviness of your secret? For example,
you might consider writing your secret
on a piece of paper and burning it.
Maybe even bury it. Maybe you go into
the woods and scream your secret into
the trees. Listen, the whole point is
just to get that thing out of you.

EVERYTHING
YOU NEED
IS RIGHT THERE
INSIDE YOU.
LET YOUR LIFE
LAUNCH YOU
INTO
YOUR DESTINY.

smile

SMILE, AND SMILE AGAIN!

There is one very low-stakes way to bless somebody: *smile!*
Honey, Tab will be in the grocery and smile at at least five
people before I'm done. Not because I'm forced to, but
because there's often power and acknowledgment in a
smile. So let's try it! Decide how many smiles you can spare
today or this week. Is it five? Ten? Now each time you smile
at someone intentionally, make a note below of where you
were and how it made you feel.

That felt good, didn't it?

Okay, now take some time to unpack any reactions you received or any reflections that came up for you after you smiled at someone.

smule

WHO ARE YOU LISTENING TO?

Some of us stay in our little boxes and are unable or unwilling to hear different points of view or learn from people who are different from us. That's not a great way to love on others. No, you don't have to agree with everything everyone says, but it doesn't hurt to hear somebody out or gain a different perspective. What are some ways you can step outside your comfort zone this week and engage with someone who is different from you?

Put one of those ways into action this week
and then reflect on what came up for you.
Were you uncomfortable?
Why do you think that is?
Were you surprised by the connection or
similarities you shared with the person?
Why do you think that happened?

WHAT'S ON YOUR MIND?

TAB CHECKS IN

"How y'all doing? Y'all alright?"

Remember, this isn't supposed to be a chore. You are free here. This is a gift you are giving to yourself. This space is yours to do with as you choose. Only you know what is coming up in you and whether you are ready to put it down on the page. This is your work alone to do. I love you!"

—TAB

BE FREE

BE FREE

BE FREE

BE FREE

BE FREE

4

Like So, Like That

BE FREE BE FREE BE
FREE BE FREE BE FREE
BE FREE
BE FREE
BE FREE
FREE BE FREE
BE FREE BE FREE
BE FREE
BE FREE

It's truly a blessing for me to know that right now, I am living and walking in complete freedom. I spent so many years trying to become someone other than Tab. Whether it was covering my accent, wearing my hair a certain way, or toning down the way I dress, I found myself doing whatever I could to fit in and be accepted. Code switching, especially for me as a Black woman, is a real thing, and I was a master of it. I thought this was the only way I could survive and be successful.

But after finding myself in that dark space of sickness, I realized that none of that was freedom. Changing who I was to make others comfortable didn't suit me at all. I had to get to the darkest place in my life to finally say, "Wait a minute, girl! You are not free. You have spent over twenty years not choosing the real you. You've been choosing whoever you thought the world wanted to see. Now you don't even know who you are anymore. Stop it. No more."

That's when I took the key and unlocked my chains.

Yes, I had the key the whole time!

Honey, let me tell you the God's honest truth: That was *no way* for anybody to live. My prayer for you is that you don't have to get sick and feel like you are going to die to realize what it took two decades for me to figure out. For the past five years, I've been getting back to Tab. Returning to the heart of that sweet, beautiful girl playing in the woods of Stoneville, North Carolina. I never again want to dishonor God by telling Him that who He made me to be wasn't enough. Because don't you know that's what we are doing when we create these other versions of ourselves? Sure, I'm an actress and in that work, I create voices and personas for my characters. But that kind of creation stays on set. When I'm Tab, I have to be Tab. When you ask for Tabitha Brown, that's who you are going to get. I'm never for sale. Baby, that's what it means to be truly free.

I want that kind of freedom for you too.

What does

freedom

mean to you?
What does it look like?

If you could write a description
of your life through

the lens of
freedom,

how would it be the same or different
from how you live today? And if you wouldn't change a
thing, well honey, very good!

The first
rule of
getting to happy,
of reclaiming
YOUR JOY,
is to put
YOURSELF
FIRST.

Two big parts of living

free

are being able to say no to the things that no longer
serve you and being able to say yes to anything that
will lead to you being as free as possible.

IN THE FIRST COLUMN,
make a list of
things you need to say no to.
IN THE SECOND COLUMN,
make a list of your yeses.

Take a minute to sit with your list.
I'm not going to tell you to make a plan just yet.
Sometimes we need time to let these shifts take hold in us.
I invite you to simply sit with what you've uncovered,
and in the space on page 132, draw whatever comes to
mind when you think about what your life will be like when
you say no or yes to those things on your list.

say no to	say yes to

MIRROR, MIRROR
ON THE WALL

Don't you know that
you are enough?

God created you special. Part of getting free means knowing that we are enough at all times. Once you settle into that, can't nobody take it away from you—not even you! You will show up in any room or space and occupy it boldly, proudly, and freely.

Set a timer for 5 minutes and spend that entire time looking at your face in the mirror. Don't look away! Stare right into those beautiful eyes of yours. In the space that follows, write what you see when you look into the mirror.
Not *just* your physical appearance, either.
Not what people have said about you or told you outright. *Not* what society and this world wants you to be. Who do *YOU* see when you shed all that outside noise?
Reflect on the mirror exercise for a bit here.
How did it make you feel to really look at yourself?

TAKE OUT THE TRASH

Now, even though I told you to tune out all those
other voices, I also know that it isn't easy to do.
Did some negative things come up when you
looked at yourself in the mirror?
Maybe some stuff that you kind of believe about
yourself, even if you really don't want to?
Write about those thoughts below.

Now let's throw that mess away, okay?

We are getting free today. Never keep those thoughts that aren't serving you. Every single time they come up, imagine this page and dump them right in the trash.

LIFE
IS TOO SHORT
BUT LIFE IS
also long
ENOUGH
if WE LIVE it
RIGHT.

Never apologize

for who you are or where you come from.
Good, bad, or indifferent, the way you grew up, the
people who raised you, helped shape who you are
today. I speak how I speak because I embrace all the
North Carolina in me. I embrace who my daddy and
mama raised me to be. In the space provided, write
the names of the places or people who shaped you—
your personality, how you see the world. Try not to
judge them. Sometimes things just are what they are.
Judging your hometown doesn't change the fact that
you were born or raised there. Judging your parents
doesn't change one day you spent in their care.
So let's get free from the chokehold our past
might be having on us:

Where/Who are you from?

_____

_____

_____

_____

_____

_____

WHAT'S ON YOUR MIND?

DO GOOD

DO GOOD

5

Very
Good

DO GOOD

DO GOOD

DO GOOD

DO GOOD

DO GOOD

DO GOOD

DO GOOD

DO GOOD

DO GOOD

DO GOOD

DO GOOD

DO GOOD

DO GOOD

DO GOOD

DO GOOD

DO GOOD

DO GOOD

DO GOOD

DO GOOD

DO GOOD

DO GOOD

DO GOOD

Nowadays, many people are wondering what it means to *do* good. To me, *doing* good is directly related to *feeling* good about what you do. Everything I do for myself and for others, I want to feel good about it. I don't want to question it. I don't want to get that icky feeling in my gut that says something isn't right. So I pay close attention to what makes me feel good in my body, mind, and spirit. I know it's common today to do things for recognition, but I do what I do in order to feel good about my existence. I need to feel good about what I'm putting out into the world.

But how can we do good if we aren't *being* good to ourselves? If we don't know what *good* feels or looks like? If we don't take care of our bodies and minds and spirits? If we've pushed our dreams and purpose aside for whatever reason?

I started my journey toward doing good in the world by being good to myself first and showing up as the best version of Tab everywhere I go. When I do that, then I can, as church folk used to say, "be about my Father's business." Being the best version of myself means checking in with my own heart to make sure my mind and spirit are together. Being the best version of myself means taking care of my body. Being the best version of myself means living in my purpose. We all have a purpose in this world. A dream we've held close to our hearts. And the best way to see our purpose fulfilled and our dreams realized is to take care of ourselves.

Here's what I know for sure: Our true purpose will always align with our dreams if we are willing to be honest with ourselves. When I was a child, my dream was to be an actress and entertainer. As I grew up and began to understand more about who I was, I realized that my purpose was to make people feel. This world will harden you if you let it. But I was born to help people become free enough to tap into the full range of their emotions. Now, sure, maybe I could have fulfilled that purpose as a psychologist or a teacher. But my dream was always to act. It didn't matter if the world or my family or my friends said, "Do this to make money" or "Go there to be successful." The work for me has always been to figure out how my dream might align with my purpose, and how I can accomplish both while being 100 percent myself.

Every time I do a video, my prayer is "God, please let people see You inside of me, so I cannot be denied." I want every viewer to get what they need. When I'm performing, it's the same way. I get to help people feel. My heart soars when I know that a character I've created has made people laugh, cry, think, or shout. For me, it feels like my work has done a small part in making people feel seen, loved, and heard. It has been the perfect alignment of my dreams and my purpose.

So let's unpack what doing good for and to yourself looks like, and how you might do good for and to others by aligning your dreams with your purpose.

Think back to when you were a kid.

Do you remember what you wanted to be when you grew up?
What about that thing you fell in love with in middle school?
That talent you uncovered in high school?

We wrote about our gifts in the first section—now let's think
more about the dreams that were birthed from those gifts.
Write a bit about those earliest dreams.

dreams

dreams

When someone asks you,
"What is your purpose?"
how do you answer? Are you honest when you answer? It's okay if your response is "I don't know," or something you've never shared with anyone before.

_____

_____

_____

_____

_____

_____

Write about what it has been like so far to

discover your purpose;

take this journey.
If you believe you know your purpose, spend some time
describing it and then unpacking how/if you are fulfilling it.

Many people do not pursue their

DREAMS AND PURPOSES

because they have bought into the lie of perfection. They think there's a right time, a right age, or a right way to achieve their dreams. Honey, I am a witness that this is not true at all! Sometimes the only thing required of you is taking the first step. Write about what your first step toward aligning your dreams with your purpose might be.

dreams

purpose

_____

_____

_____

_____

_____

_____

_____

_____

It's scary to let go of the perfection excuse.
We ask ourselves, what if we mess up?
What if we get it wrong? Okay, what if?
Write out the

worst-case scenario

of taking your first step toward living your best life.

Now write your
best-case scenario.

_____

_____

_____

_____

_____

_____

_____

... the things
we keep inside,
they grow.
you deserve
to be free from it.
you owe yourself
the freedom
so you can
breathe again.

SPREAD *love*

IT'S THE TAB WAY

You've probably heard me say this a million times, so one more time won't hurt. My intent every day is to spread love. To be good to people. That's it! Doing good for ourselves, for the people around us, and for the world as a whole starts with setting an intention at the start of every day to do exactly that.

NOW, HOW DO I DO THAT, TAB?

I know, I know. We hear people say "Set your intention" all the time, and there are a million different definitions out there. Let Tab make it easy for you. Setting an intention simply means you are intentionally deciding what your mindset and action for the day will be.

For the next seven days,

take 5 minutes every morning to sit still and set your intention for the day. It can be whatever you want. For example, maybe you want to focus on actively listening to your loved ones and friends. That's great! When you wake up in the morning, go to a quiet place and sit with your decision to talk less and listen more. See yourself doing it. If you pray, ask God to help you do it. Then go about your day. I've provided space on the next two pages for you to write your intention each day and then reflect on the outcome, if any, at the end of the day.

Day 1—Intention _____

Reflect on your Day 1 intention. _____

_____

_____

Day 2—Intention _____

Reflect on your Day 2 intention. _____

_____

_____

Day 3—Intention _____

Reflect on your Day 3 intention. _____

_____

_____

Day 4—Intention

Reflect on your Day 4 intention. _____

_____

_____

Day 5—Intention

Reflect on your Day 5 intention. _____

_____

_____

Day 6—Intention

Reflect on your Day 6 intention. _____

_____

_____

Day 7—Intention

Reflect on your Day 7 intention. _____

_____

_____

THERE ARE MULTIPLE ROUTES TO ANY DESTINATION.

It's way too easy, especially with social media, to get caught up in other people's dreams and get confused about our own dreams. We can get so fixated on somebody else's life—what they're doing and how they're doing it—that we think that's what *we* should do. We make their accomplishment our goal. *That's* not good. *That's* how we miss out on opportunities to discover our purpose.

Let's release our distractions.

Make a list of ten things

you know get in the way of you pursuing your dreams and discovering your purpose.

1. _____

2. _____

3. _____

4. _____

5. _____

6. _____

7. _____

8. _____

9. _____

10. _____

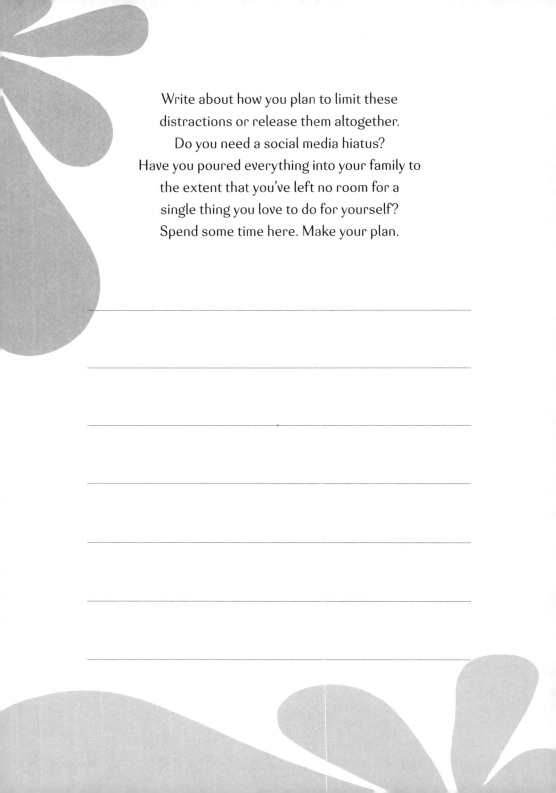

Write about how you plan to limit these distractions or release them altogether. Do you need a social media hiatus? Have you poured everything into your family to the extent that you've left no room for a single thing you love to do for yourself? Spend some time here. Make your plan.

After we've done the work to consider how we might be better to ourselves in order to be better for others, there is one important question we must ask:

Are we really ready to live in purpose?

Because part of being ready means being okay with people not understanding what we are doing, or not receiving us even when we're trying to do good. We must not allow ourselves to be affected by others. As you wrap up this leg of your journaling journey, take some time to reflect on how you will stay the course. How will you choose yourself every single time and continue to pursue your dreams, even if, in the short term, you can't see the impact those choices are having?

WHAT'S ON YOUR MIND?

HOW Y'ALL DOING?
Y'ALL ALRIGHT?

Congratulations! Look at you! Honey, finishing this journal is a huge step toward finding your freedom. To seeing yourself, hearing yourself, and loving yourself. I'm so very proud of you for making the choice to do that. My hope is that once you feel you are 100 percent in love with yourself and caring for yourself as you should, then and only then will you go and spread that love to others.

Invite others into your journey. Share with them the love that you've found for yourself. Feel free to share this journal with them and maybe even share some of the exercises that helped you. And as I've been saying, it's okay if not every exercise helped. Maybe there's just one that really sticks out in your mind as one that impacted you. Go on 'head and share that joy with a friend or family member. Hopefully, as you continue to grow, you'll return to some of what you've read and written here and remind yourself of how far you've come. There's a reason why you started this and there's a reason why you finished. Knowing your "why" and revisiting that why gives you the encouragement to love yourself even more. It's so important that we remind ourselves of what we've *been* through so that we have a better sense of what we are *going* through (in the present) and how to move *forward* (in the future).

You know Tab loves you, right? And I hope that throughout this process, you feel seen and heard. Most of all, I hope that you feel understood. You are not alone. You have a sister, friend, mama, or auntie in me and I'm rooting for you. At the end of all this, I pray that you do something new. Apply for that job. Audition for that role. Make that phone call. See that person you've been avoiding. You can do it. You are so brave.

Be all that you've ever wanted to be. You are enough.

'Love, Tab

DON'T LET
YOUR
SITUATION NOW
DETERMINE
HOW YOU WILL
LIVE YOUR
LIFE FOREVER.